I0223674

Pasadena Rose Poets Poetry Collection 2019

Reflection. Resistance. Reckoning. Resurrection.

Editor-in-Chief:

Gerda Govine Ituarte

Pasadena Rose Poets Poetry Collection 2019

Copyright © 2019 by Gerda Govine Ituarte

All rights reserved. No part of this book may be reproduced or transmitted in any form or by any means without written permission of the author.

Library of Congress Control Number: 2019948399

ISBN: 978-0-9600931-3-7

Published by Shabda Press
Pasadena, CA 91107
www.shabdapress.com

Introduction

The Pasadena Rose Poets are "unobtrusive pause creators." We use our words to allow humanity to pause and breathe deeply. Poetry leaves its mark—not always visible—but imprinted on us and our audience in ways that we may never know. We are a chorus of voices stretched across cultures. Poetry gifts us with a third eye and ear that slows us down to look and see, to hear murmurs and whispers that get under our skin and live in our heads until we let the words land on the page. We fly, soar as time, space and freedom joins us.

An NEA, National Endowment for the Arts, grant to the City of Pasadena Cultural Affairs Division created the winds of change that established The Pasadena Rose Poets in 2016. Nine published poets were chosen to initiate a lunchtime poetry reading program at the Pasadena Senior Center in 2016 and in the Pasadena Council Chambers in 2018. We are also know as "Citizen Poets," who initiated and continued to read at City Council meetings since 2017. As Mayor Terry Tornek remarked at one of the Council meetings, *I believe that because of the poetry readings, the meetings are more civil.*

Acknowledgment

Rochelle Branch, Director, City of Pasadena Cultural Affairs Division; Emily Hopkins, Director Side Street Projects; Christine Reeder, Senior Librarian, Adult Services, Pasadena Central Library; Pasadena Mayor Terry Tornek, Pasadena City Councilmember John J. Kennedy; Vice Mayor Tyron Hampton; Marcia Arrieta and Victor Vazquez, former Pasadena Rose Poets; Book Show Bookstore; Poets Don Kingfisher and Thelma Reyna; Luis Ituarte, Artist; LitFest Pasadena; and Alfred Haymond, Photographer.

In Memory Of

Godfather Jose Antonio Jarvis, Renaissance man, the first poet in my life.

Jaylene Mosley a too-soon-departed Sister Friend, May 25, 2019.

Call To All Poets

I call all poets of our country to undertake a campaign so that the importance of the arts in the welfare of our society is not forgotten. One of the critical civic events in the nation is a city council meeting held numerous times per month. This is where citizens have an opportunity to speak directly to and with their councilmembers and other government officials.

In Pasadena, California a group of "Citizen Poets," The Pasadena Rose Poets, took the initiative to recite poetry during the three-minute public comment portion, which is granted to each citizen. This encourages civic leaders to think about the significance of art to develop a more humane and healthy society. These poetic interventions are simply to utilize the three minutes in this way to ensure it is an on-going part of the citizen's conversation.

CALLING ALL THE POETS OF THE COUNTRY to take possession of these three minutes in the name of art, thus forming a national movement to integrate art as an essential part of our cultural experience.

Luis Ituarte, Artist
Pasadena Rose Poets Advisor

Group collage

Contents

Gerda Govine Ituarte

1

After the Fire

Things broken cracked gone
      rolled family pictures to curb
        residue of life lived
            fear sadness whiff of hope
               walk back to new normal.

Gerda Govine Ituarte

Alabama Bound on the Jim Crow Line

Grandma often told
the story
of taking my mother,
her daughter
and my mother's brothers,
grandma's sons
to
Mobile, Alabama
in summer
riding white
first class
travelling to the mouth
of the South
Mobile, Alabama
on the Jim Crow Line.

At summer's end
with sunburned skin
mama and her brothers
no longer white
all rode black
going back
the train holding course
travelling North
on the Jim Crow Line.

Toni Mosley

Aqua Frames

New aqua glasses frame her face
      as she peers out

          in style

Her blue eyes sparkle
      like the ocean glazed over

Aqua has set in
      spread to her latest finds

Blouse immersed
      in field of flowers

Rhinestones sequins
      stretch out into her life

Becoming aqua
          like
          night music.

Gerda Govine Ituarte

Kate Gale

Aristotle's Catfish

My song-fish
My joy bite

Cornmeal, thyme
crisp fin, of tail

Bones to the cat
who licks and crunches.

Kate Gale

Beasts

(for 8-year-old Asifa Bano, killed in Kathua, India, in January 2018)

It wasn't your fault,
their madness is a disease as ancient
as the sickness it brings,
the beasts caught you in
that moment when angels stepped away,
your prayers unheard, your screams muffled
by the darkness in their merciless minds

your screams echoed to a wounded world,
one that begs your forgiveness,
that pleads for your understanding
that humankind is blind to those
who are precious like you,
who reminds us of what we might be
if we found courage to face the hostility
and ugliness of who we are,
living apart but together on the blade of insanity

the beasts still slither among us, their fears
shaped as brutal beliefs and hazy ignorance,
and in your final breaths and thoughts,
I hope you realized a truth more enduring than gold:
the beasts that tortured your innocent body,
could never steal any part of your infinite soul

Mel Donalson

Bike Accident

My closest encounter with a rose
bush was when I crashed into one.
While a child and riding my bike,
I thought I would challenge myself –
pedal fast, let go of my feet and hands.
Then, I lost control and went straight into
a rose bush. The bike on top of me, thorns
in my body. Flesh cut and bleeding.
The rose entered my bloodstream
and eyelids scattered over me.

I guess it was then, as when Peter Parker was
bitten by a spider and became Spiderman–when I became a poet.

Teresa Mei Chuc

Biology 1A

Dear Miss Saccoman, you made me
sit in the backroom next to the skeleton
because I distracted freckled Margie,

the albino football player with specs,
and you. Your cluttered periodic table
or the video on the mitosis of onion root

drove me near suicide. I screamed
in anger, "I don't want to be a scientist
when I grow up!" You nodded and erased

the blackboard full of evolution.
Dust fell. "I want to become a writer,"
I said. You nodded and led me

to the back, to the toothless skeleton,
smiled, sharpened my shriveled pencil,
and asked me to write.

Shahé Mankerian

Published in The Metonym, *Uninhibited* thematic edition, 2015.
Published in Altadena Poetry Review Anthology 2015.

Blue Light from the TV

Love is snacking in bed
in front of late night TV
then when the snacks are gone
and the show is over and
It's silently dark
and we're skin on skin,
you kiss and hold and
make love to me while
whispering "I love you, baby."

The blue light from the TV
is like love floating on a blue moon.

Toni Mosley

Body of Water

Flows
back and forth

Body of Water
drinks me in

Body of Water
thirsty no more

Body of water
this holy body mine.

Gerda Govine Ituarte

Damian Gonzalez

Bottle

I think of you often
You are younger in my dreams—delicate
eyes detailed with a craftsmanship long lost at sea
like the last hopes of a dried banana leaf scroll
harboring tales written in blood by a castaway
about peach skies and ocean bodies; hearts and time
sealed tight inside a sand-washed bourbon bottle
corked and fated to bow against the current one day
and float with it the next.

Damian Gonzalez

Bubble

A family of bubbles bloom from the tip of an easy-action cap
atop a bottle of dishwashing detergent
that I squeezed while washing dishes.

An infinitesimal representation of the big bang—
a miracle.

I have never witnessed a miracle before.

The beginning floats gently in front of me
and everything falls away
while effervescent life spawns.

Worlds of cool air capsules ride currents of my breath,
disperse, and become the cosmos.

For a moment I am God.

Some number describing how fast light travels through them
would explain why they look like mini-rainbows
but I don't know that number.

Tiny fragile soapy membranes cradle ambivalence,
the only thing separating light-heartedness from tragedy—

Pop!

Damian Gonzalez

Calligraphy

When I learned to write,
my mother began with the elements:

Earth   土
and fire   火
water   水
and wood 木.

Then,
the sky   天,
its sun   日
and moon 月,
clouds   云,
and rain   雨.

Brush to black ink, our hands
traversing the smooth page.

My mother's voice,
her guiding hand

painting the world
in bold strokes.

Annette Wong

Published version, Altadena Poetry Review 2017.

Group Photo

Coin Op

Bleak morning; misty constant rain, penetrating cold.
Cement mouse-trap; a strip mall housing Carnicería, Donut Shop, Chinese
food for a buck, and a Coin-Op Laun-dro-mat—the ante meridiem refuge.
Men in one-piece jumpsuits blue in the collar, grimace at losing lottery tickets.
Mothers, some without visas or passports, or rent for this month,
or a fix for this moment pray blessings under a grey sky for sons and daughters
they won't see again for a long time.
Box-sheltered veterans mutter something about GI checks.
Moths and mosquitos circle the sodium vapor security lights.
Caucasian artists with handlebar moustaches feel alive here—
On the corner are the best tacos in town.
Nearby, an art-loft; inside it is warm despite having eighteen-foot
high cement walls.
Living there: Thrift-shop clothing clad Jane Doe (aficionado of social justice)
Jane plays dress-up, bicycles around refuting nepotism, and refuses to eat meat.
Jane is nice, she and her boyfriend insist that they are not above anyone
but that everyone here has already laid down.
It's not their fault they've inherited racism, ethnocentrism, elitism,
an absence of skin pigment, no chill in the bones, and no growling in the belly.
Bleak morning; scornful, mocking morning.
It is cold and my hands hurt.
The sun rises with no rays,
just a marine-layer cascading light particles across an entire neighborhood,
no one sure if it is time to rise—no one really sure if it's time to be awake.
Upon rising early, I feel a profound sadness.

Damian Gonzalez

Conversation with an Evergreen

Along
the road
I met an old evergreen
Her crown brushed the sky
Her trunk forked into three strong branches
Her roots sank deep in the earth.
Chile, where you goin in such a hurry?
Why don't you stop and rest a spell?
"Sorry, I ain't got time," I said pausing to admire her odd shape
A blue jay landed on one of her limbs
She listened to its chatter then focused her eyes on me
Sometimes you get more done bein' still than you do runnin' around
I been standin' in this same spot for over a hundred years and I bet
I get more done in one hour than you do in a whole life time
Her trunk invited me to sit
As I rested in her lap her pine scent cleared my head
Just 'cause y'all humans don't hear trees talk don't mean we can't
We got all kinds of phone lines underground
Know how I make it through a storm? she chuckled
I let go of dead branches so I can bend in the wind
Sometimes you gotta let thangs go
I sat for a while listening
To the whoosh of wind whispering
through her leaves
Heading home
I realized
I learned more
from her in one hour
than I learned from all my years in schools.

Hazel Clayton Harrison

Corned Beef and Cabbage and Mama's Depression

I remember when I used to phone my mother checking up on her every Sunday morning when I began to note that every call was being met with her response of "Oh, Baby, I'm feeling blue today" or that she was down in the dumps and couldn't understand why. Later I learned too late that she was suffering from depression, symptomatic of the aging process.

To offset her depression and put a smile on her face, I would immediately change the conversation to food. Sunday mornings was when I would try to plan Sunday dinners. In her day, mama had been a great cook and kept her recipes in an index card file. So, my ploy for calling was to get her recipe for things such as fried chicken, greens or red beans and rice. Foods I already knew how to cook. The last call I made was for her recipe of corned beef and cabbage on October 28, 1999, the day before her 75th birthday. I remembered the fun we had laughing, talking and struggling to remember when.

"You're cooking corned beef and cabbage? How odd," she laughed. "I never imagined anyone in your house wanting to eat such an old fashioned meal." I laughed, too, and told her "yes, we eat old fashioned meals in my house, like your delicious corned beef and cabbage and rye bread. It's the only way my kids will eat cabbage." She laughed, reminding me how I hated that meal when I was a kid. I reminded her that I was grown now and that my palate had changed.

Chuckling, she said "Okay, I'll go get the recipe." I heard her lay the phone down giggling as she slowly made her way to the kitchen for her recipe box. She surprised me at the quickness of her return to the phone. "Okay, kiddo, here you go," as she slowly read ingredients, cooking times and the type of rye bread I should serve. I didn't know it then but aging brought on a sense of uselessness but I guess her recipe box was feeling pretty useless, too, since Mama didn't cook much anymore, except when I called begging for instructions of how to cook whatever I had planned that day.

I told her I'd bring her leftovers tomorrow for lunch. "We will celebrate your birthday, too," I promised. "Oh baby, I know parents aren't supposed to have favorites, but you were always mine. So loving and responsible."

The next day I arrived at 12 noon and she was in a snit about getting ready for a trip to Las Vegas to meet her beloved. She announced that they were getting married and that he was picking her up at 12:30. "And who are you?" she suspiciously queried, staring as though I were a stranger.

Mama was mentally in the year 1960 preparing for her second marriage; but sometime after our phone conversation the day before and this moment when I was now a stranger, I knew something was seriously wrong. I had to get her to the hospital. So I lied and told her that her fiancé had phoned and said he would pick her up at Mercy Hospital. He worked nearby and was anxious to see his bride-to be.

What I learned was that yesterday her Alzheimer's disease had waited for her to finish her conversation with me then had stealthy moved in before I could bring her corned beef and cabbage for lunch. When the doctor gave his prognosis, I knew it was too late to eat cake and blow out her single candle.

Toni Mosley

Dad's 80th Birthday

Dad's doctor visit
bad news
lung cancer stage 4

Admitted into hospital
surgery bed rest
chemo prescribed

Plans already underway
for his 80th surprise
birthday party

What to do?
cancel or go ahead?
decide not to cancel

Day after discharge
house humming
balloons   banners
food   gifts
lemon cake (his favorite)
family friends arrive

Help Dad downstairs
Surprise!
Look on his face
priceless

Laughter hugs tears
his first and last
birthday party

Best medicine.

Hazel Clayton Harrison

Dear Grandfather

In that old photo you look so proud
in your Sunday-go-to-meeting suit
Your face, solemn as a country preacher
      thick moustache trimming your upper lip
      eyes looking as if they could see the storms ahead.

Now I see how you stole Big Momma's heart
Your spade hands dug up barrels of clay
      turned them into bales of cotton
      reached up plucked stars from the sky
      stroked the moon.

My mother said angels wept, heavens parted
      when you prayed.

The year before my seed sprouted from her garden, your long legs
      leaped over rainbows
      crossed the River Jordan
      headed home to Calvary.

Now I grow in soil you
      plowed
      watered
      planted.

I never sat on your lap or called you Grandpa
but one day we'll meet and walk hand-in-hand
into the rising sun.

Hazel Clayton Harrison

Dear Mama

Yesterday
a yellow flower
burst from the
prickly pear
on the
back porch

Its petals
unfolded
so gracefully
from its bed
of thorns

I couldn't help
but think
of you.

Hazel Clayton Harrison

Dear Page

You accept me as I am
tattered and confused
stumbling over words
and rocks
when I am in tears

You accept
my heart and being

How this blankness
the color of cloud
and winged milkweed
seeds
could hold my soul
completely
without judgment

Here is my home.

Teresa Mei Chuc

Delayed Choice Quantum Erasure

My father wanted for me milk.
My mother wanted for me god.
They took me to the milk place,
the god place, the yum place.

And stars they wanted for me
Stars burned out long ago.
Shooting stars throwing light streams,
dead rock falling through heat

My father wanted for me milk
He said to Mother, Stay with her.
Don't put on heels and work Wall Street.
Don't be a doctor or a physicist.

After the rape, Father couldn't see me.
Dr. Asesino said, She will never have children
Not after this.
Not after this so young.

Mother made this move when I came in the room.
Like flies were buzzing, she brushed air. Quantum erasure
means you might not yet ever exist in this universe
You hang like a shadow here.

Then you appear in another story, another universe.
In that world, I'm a comet, I take on the night sky.

Kate Gale

Hazel Clayton Harrison

27

Doombo and Skilletpeg

(for my brother)

In the back woods of Georgia where we were born in a cabin
        he was called Doombo and I was Skilletpeg.

Who gave us those nicknames and why I'll never know
it was like being named after a comedy duo
        like Laurel and Hardy or Amos n' Andy.

When we moved up North nobody called us that anymore.
We were simply two colored kids growing up on the North end of town
        trying to figure out who we were and where we were going.

In our teenaged years we became obsessed with our bodies
he took up body building; I dreamed of fashion modeling
        but dreams die hard in the ghetto.

After high school he followed our father's footsteps into the mill
Afraid I would be lured into a wolf's den, my mother
        sent me away to school to become a teacher.

When we were little he and I didn't get along
but as my older brother, he always towered over me like a mountain
        a mountain I could never fathom or scale
        a mountain I had to look up to and learn to accept
        and appreciate for its grandeur and power
        a mountain with wide shoulders that heaved over the Valley

and endured life's harsh winds and storms.

Hazel Clayton Harrison

Doused Dolması

Her husband didn't allow the coroner
to remover her dress. The rotating fan

hummed overhead and spread the smell
of sweet onions from his wife's satchel.

She was returning from the bazaar.
The flickering fluorescent mimicked

his trembling hand. He clutched the dirty
rag and dabbed her chin; blood stains

took the shape of a kiss. The bullet
had entered her left cheek and lodged

underneath her skull. A ballet of flies
distracted his gaze. "And for dinner,

what would you like?" She had asked
subserviently. He replayed his command

regretfully: "*Soğan Dolması.*" He knew
she never failed to overstuff the onions

with meat and rice to near suffocation.

Shahé Mankerian

Annette Wong

Drama

David Mamet says

there is no such thing
as character.

Only things people do
and say.

Drama is plot. Everything
in service of story.

All utterances: myths.
Lies.

If an incident fails to further
the story, cut it out.

Like a joke,
all good

drama tends towards
the punch

line.

Annette Wong

Published version Altadena Poetry Review 2018.

Entomology

(the ant and the grasshopper)

Fall: there was time, still, after
a summer squandered in song.
The scythes still whistled
the fruit still hung – so he danced
after the cicadas had gone.

And as she had, all summer long
tried to warn (he paid no heed)
with jaws clenched, mined
what she could, what she had
What more could she do?

We know how the story goes: winter.
A first frost. A rattling wind.
No grass, no song, no swarm (one
is the loneliest locust).

Hobbling now, at her nest's foot
His feeble shrill. Silence. And then –
an antennae's twitch (her knowing
look) that all familiar
refrain: "Don't say
I didn't tell you so."

Annette Wong

Published version Spark and Echo Arts 2013.

Found: on Graph Paper

1) The heat

    2) The sadness,

        3) Surrounded by boxes

4) Under water

    5) She's fallen

        6) Off the grid.

Carla Sameth

Funeral

Her body was round in places most women work endlessly to conceal, to thin, or to remove altogether.

She had a fullness that filled palms and outstretched fingers taught with lust for it;

Her contours demanded knowledge of calligraphy—skilled hands, capable of creating elegant loops and gentle italic letters joined at each and every end, to form words neither gentle nor blasphemous but simultaneously spiritual and condemning.

Often more whiskey than woman, one night while drinking down divinity I watched her black-light heart glow violet against white Egyptian cotton.

She laid her head down and left lives unlived, dreams unfulfilled, and memories too painful to take with her in the morning—she left poetry.

in cars parked from view
you savor finite moments
because love comes fast

lust stretched on window
showing neighbors, you were starved
but love don't live here

drunk under moon-shine
you fall and laugh at yourself
love like bed, broken

Her bourbon words scrawled across sheets of truths—
Of all the languages spoken amongst women and men,
verses she wrote were the most comforting.

That night she taught me that there are beautiful things in this world,
and there are sad things in this world, and no one can be sure which there
is more of.

"The mind…" she said, "is not interested in morality
and the dead don't carry the burden of mistakes,
so fuck me and kill me, and let tomorrow be better."
And so I did. And it was.

Damian Gonzalez

Group Photo

Grandma (A Hologram)

In your physical absence,
the hologram of me
still contains you
like a cut leaf –
you are part of the light
scattered from me so that even
a tiny fragment, an eyelash,
will still contain the whole of you.

Teresa Mei Chuc

Hear/Say

You say, You're pretty.
I hear, I want you naked

You say, Let's meet later for a drink.
I hear, Let's fuck.

I hear, Dick.
You say, Let me tell you about my…

*

You say, You take my breath away.
I hear, Give me a blowjob.

You say, We had an instant attraction.
I hear, I knew you'd give in.

I hear, Goodbye.
You say, I'll call you.

Kate Gale

Hugging My Grandma

This is how it feels
to hold a peach tree. Not
the trunk of the tree,
but the branches. The branches
full of leaves and blossoms
and me just holding them.
The bees circle to get
pollen and nectar,
so in my arms
are bees and butterflies
and fragrance and the assurance
of fruits. O how the branches
tremble with so many open arms.

Teresa Mei Chuc

Toni Mosley

Hypnosis

My bedroom window was always
open at the ½-inch crack inviting
trance-inducing air to hypnotize
me to sleep at wintertime.

The air always frigid,
crawled in next to where I slept
but made warm with
blankets piled high
cocooning under a mother's love,

Silence filled the atmosphere as
the black sky shone with stars
brilliantly lighting the street's floor

Crystals gently falling, tapping the leaves
of the tall oaks in the vacant lot
next door

I inhaled the frigid draft
as its hypnotic cold put
me in a trance waiting
for sleep to come

I remember waking
yet never feeling
the frost of Minus One.

Toni Mosley

I Am An Immigrant

City Council chambers packed
mothers fathers sons daughters aunties uncles
hearts pound fear hope frustration
mark their faces voices rise

What does courage look like   This is what courage looks like
What does democracy look like   This is what democracy looks like

Lives stitched together with threads of resistance
stuck in concrete shadows and chain-linked dreams
life buckles under everyday threat of arrest deportation
use our words influence intellect

What does courage look like   This is what courage looks like
What does democracy look like   This is what democracy looks like

Because we struggle we gain strength
because there is no light we learn to see in the dark
our voices bring freedom from inside out
came with nothing—this country gave us everything

What does courage look like   This is what courage looks like
What does democracy looks like   This is what democracy looks like

We will stand with you   if you stand with us
We will have your back   if you have our backs.

Gerda Govine Ituarte

Inherited Legacies

Here is what I inherited from my family:
The love of alcohol. Daddy loved Jack Daniels. Scotch, water back. At night. Mama loved Smirnoff Vodka and orange juice. Morning, noon and night. I love wine. No special brand. Whatever's on hand.
Mama and her four brothers were heavy drinkers. My husband complains I'm not far behind.

Then there's the threat of disease—
Cancer—the Big C
Daddy's daddy had it
Daddy's sister had it
Daddy's brother had it
Mama's mama had it
My sister had it
I had it and am the lone survivor I'm proud to say.

Then there's the Sugar—as diabetes was called back in the day.
Mama's brother lost a foot then a leg then his mind.

We had no church. No religion. Daddy had quarrels with religion. Mama had quarrels with daddy about religion. I married a man with quarrels around religion. Mama's mama had no quarrels with religion. She was Pentecostal. That scared me. So I've had quarrels with religion. No family church, no family bible, and never learned to pray.

And…Then there was trauma.

Daddy's brother killed his wife then himself. Left two babies crying.
Daddy killed himself. The black news said he was despondent.
The white news said nothing. Back then blacks were no news.
My uncle's son was shot and killed as he slept.

1960 was the year I just wept and wept.

Toni Mosley

In Praise of Emptiness

I am looking for what's not there:
that space we look through,
the curve of a bowl,
a window.
Blankness on paper:
the smooth white
between words,
between lines,
what is not said,
what is not done.
The hollow in a bird's bones.

When someone looks at my palms,
it's as if I'm holding nothing
but the world.

Teresa Mei Chuc

Mel Donalson

Interpretation

what happens when the trigger is squeezed,
a life changed and transformed,
no raising from the dead, no apologies can return
a stolen soul, leaving an unfinished song,
a void of possibilities hurled off into eternity,

children who will no longer play,
teens who will no longer dance,
women, too soon, forced beneath the mortician's hand,
men, too often, sinking in lakes of blood and indifference

we, the civilized, taking refuge in a twenty-word
phrase, bowing at its assumed perfection,
yet forgetting that those who wrote the words were
imperfectly weak, and were not gods
but fumbling fathers of a particular hue,
who worshipped power and
amended freedom to fit
only their skin,
only their class,
only their vision where
diversity was a sin
and importance resided only in themselves

our legacy maintains this illusion
of gentility, where tears must
flow beneath an ideal that
holds no sanity or salvation,

47

reducing the nation to a rumbling
and grumbling of the illogical and
delusional who choose to shoot and subtract,
rather than to change and create,

leaving us in a land of misery,
each waiting our turn
when we all must bleed

Mel Donalson

Intersection

The last time I tasted joy,
I walked along Crystal Cove,*
stretching my thoughts in sandy strides,
indulging the sun's caress
as my ankles kissed the changing tides

the last time I touched love,
celebrating with my wife and son,
laughter the grace over a savored meal,
falling into the moment's serenity,
hungrily inhaling all that I could feel

the last time I embraced hope,
I stood at the edge of the world,
the South African sunset at Cape Agulhas,**
strangers sharing rogue waves in wonder
that peace could roar like whispering thunder

Mel Donalson

*A California state beach and park north of Laguna Beach
** The southern tip of South Africa where the Atlantic and Indian oceans meet

In the City of Roses

the homed
and the homeless
their bones curl
in the same
sleeping positions
under a black sky

waking
in a new year
on Colorado Blvd.

with Monarch butterflies
made of roses.

Teresa Mei Chuc

Jacaranda

When I first arrived in Los Angeles, I was in awe of so many things. Like signs that said Miracle Mile, Koreatown or Bungalow Heaven but what turned me from a voyeur to a lover was the bursting out of the Jacarandas. Purple fireworks lining the streets every season sometimes later than another. But no matter what had or hadn't happened the Northridge Earthquake, another miscarriage, El Nino and cars floating down lumpy cracked streets where money wasn't spent on street repair.

No matter what, those Jacarandas burst into view, not just one, but all, up and down the streets, in South Pasadena, the Mayberry of San Gabriel Valley, in Hacienda Heights the first spot for those fleeing the East LA barrios, or in West LA, where long curled tendrils of hair adorned little Jewish Orthodox children. They too stroll past the Jacarandas.

One day I saw the bougainvillea on our block that twisted in and out of the Jacaranda. I'd vowed I'd never live without bougainvillea, that the next time I moved, there would be full purple fuchsia of years covering the landscape in front of wherever I'd sleep.

The next year the Jacaranda blossomed with the red bougainvillea intertwined deep and unavoidable I felt this gift of spring. This too, is my home, because I can count on you to return every year. What was lost, the family, the stepdaughter, the security of the big house with the growing bougainvillea? Divorce couldn't take away that knowledge that I too will return, because *this* Jacaranda on *this* street hugging *this* bougainvillea belongs to everyone.

Carla Sameth

Journey

Uncover the city's hidden
      qualities
      areas for improvement
urge creativity
      artists do not yell shout
      our work speaks in its own voice
bring unexpected
      surprises that trigger change
      moments of laughter
feeling stuck   overwhelmed
      by beauty that captures
      knowing that our creativity
is shared again and again
      even when lights are turned off
      our eyelids may close
our eyes are open
      images glide by revealing the
      wonder that we draw from.

Gerda Govine Ituarte

Published in "Poetry Within Reach in Unexpected Places, "DesEscondido/
No Longer Hidden," Exhibit, California Center for the Arts Museum
Escondido, CA, October 2018.

Teresa Mei Chuc

Killing the Mekong River

I trace my finger along
the long blue curving river on the map,
running through five countries:
from the Lasagongma Spring
in the Tibetan Plateau in China,
through Myanmar, Laos, Thailand,
Cambodia and ending
in the Mekong Delta in Vietnam,
the river's fingers reaching into
the South China Sea.

The Irrawaddy dolphin,
the giant softshell turtle, the giant catfish,
the sarus crane of the Mekong River
are critically endangered and nearly extinct
from overfishing, pollution,
the building of dams
and loss of habitat.

Seven dams are depriving the river
of its life-giving floods,
and there are plans for twenty-seven dams.
There is so much that is dying.
Rivers are meant to breathe.

The saola, mythical unicorn,
is nearly extinct from deforestation
in the Mekong.

Millions of people,
fishermen and villagers,
depend on the Mekong River's flow.
Flooding of the delta brings
in nutrients from upstream
for rice farmers in Vietnam.
Wetland reeds are used for basketry.

River canoes, floating market boats.

What will be gone with the river?
I look at a photograph of a man carrying his small son
in his arm as he walks the cracked and dry bottom
of the Mekong Delta.

Teresa Mei Chuc

L'l Woo's Eulogy for his Mama

The Angel
of Death
called Mama
home yesterday
but she got
ninety good years in
did her own thang
lived in her own house
cooked her own food
drove her own Caddie
on the highway at 55 miles per hour
raised all eight of us
me bein' the baby
and the baddest
she toe' my butt up
taught me to drive
on the hardest
roads.

Hazel Clayton Harrison

Medusa's Cookbook

Thin layers of pastry
like grasshopper's wings
salt
Almond paste
nutmeg
Cloves—an unopened flower bud
Cinnamon—a spiraled brown quill
Honey
Crushed nuts.

Kate Gale

Medusa in Love

You start off young and beautiful; things go wrong.
That's my life. That's any life.

My father used to say, smile when you come into a room.
When I come into a room and see men, I smile.

The suitors line up for me. Boys and men.
Never a fan of beards. Hairy men are a no.

Mother says, Don't act like that, they'll call you a bitch.
Like what? I say. Like a bitch, she says.

At parties, I dance. The doors of the world opening.
Windows too. Whom will I will marry?

My smiling works on everyone, but eventually I have to choose.
When you're young, pretty, smiling, there is everyone to choose from.

Ask Ovid, ask anyone.
I was raped in the temple of Athena.

After rape, everything changes. What were you doing?
Did you struggle? Did you try to get away? What were you wearing?

Did you wear red? Did you wear heels? Was your clothing too tight?
Did you show neck, ankle, belly, wrist?

Poseidon held me against the white columns in his monstrous hands.
He raped me on the floor of the temple.

If you are raped in church, it's hard to go back to church,
talk to God. It's obvious God doesn't listen to you.

I heard children playing on the shore.
Sunlight poured through the white temple.

Everyone attended a party that night. My suitors were there.
Too bad, they said. They danced with other girls.

Don't ask me what happened next. Athena's curse.
The years huddled dark. My hair turned a vile nest of vipers.

I grew hair everywhere. Women are not supposed to have hair
except on their heads and that head hair should be contained.

The men who had wanted to bed me, competed to shoot me.
Pierce me with swords. Throw spears. Throw knives.

Killing Medusa cartoons were the rage. You could say anything about me.
Throw bottles. Break glass. I absorbed all human rage.

I had not only my own snake, but many snakes.
I had the power to kill men.

O Perseus, you rescued me from torment.
I will be born again. I will have a new name.

Kate Gale

Medusa's Mother

*The lesson from tragedy is that when women are removed from their natural environment of the household (**oikos**) and come to occupy any sort of prominent position in the city (**polis**), then they become most dangerous.* Sam Newington on Greek society

Hemmed in by fire.
Someday I'll have husband and daughters.
After I give up

I'm still clothes-lining
bread baking for my father
I want to lead.

To emote fire, to change Greece.
We want everything men have. Not their bodies.
We want power.

The men laugh. She can't even get a husband.
Poor thing. Nobody wants her.
There she goes spitting out words.

Nobody wants the words of a woman.
They're chaff, scattered to the winds.
In a circle, men talk.

Money, boats, scaffolding.
Houses, roads, bridges.
Wheat, corn, silver, gold.

I join the circle, throw
out new subjects.
Healing and bread.

The gulls wheel overhead.
The men turn to each other
as if I haven't spoken.

Sometimes one will pick up my words
repeat them, get a round of applause.
For my words from his mouth.

Thought patterns create words,
create ideas. Create change. Seagulls
eat my words as they fall to the ground.

The thrash of bed, of corn, of children
the proper sphere for women,
not the public

where her eye can rove
the machinations of her
devious brain can revel.

Women collect around barrels of rainwater.
Our words so much water spilling on our feet.
Our thoughts spin into bread and washing.

Finally I marry the man.
While I hang out clothes to dry.
I watch ships leave the harbor

Could the philosopher king
Be a woman?
Must all leaders be brutes?

Kate Gale

Shahé Mankerian

Midnight Snack

To my students I say, "Go outside
and climb the tilted trellis to the roof.

The finch's nest is not secure
next to the waterspout. Step over it

gingerly like a beetle pawing the sprout
of moss before sinking. Like Jesus,

pretend the wave of the ceramic shingles
is your Sea of Galilee. The chimney

like a chaise will support your tired shoulders.
Lean against it. Let your gaze be fixed

on the glaze of the midnight blanket.
Tuck yourself in. The full moon will ascend

like a donut hole in the sky,
squint your eyes, and take a bite."

Shahé Mankerian

Carla Sameth

Mornings Still Scare Me

If I had a wish
it would be to jump out of bed like
the world was on fire, raining ice-cream sundaes.

My body weeping with my wife's caresses. My heart tattooed
with my son's sweet love. My sides aching
from laughter that tastes like sweet jalapeño jelly.

Carla Sameth

Bitchin' Kitsch Zine, March 2018.

Mother, Father, Mistress

Let that whore at the pastry shop percolate
your father's black coffee with cardamom.

Let her drizzle sizzling syrup on the *kadaif.*
Maybe he'll choke on the powdered pistachio,

crushed without love. Her chador never covers
her tattooed cleavage; your father eyes them

like a pair of *baba au rhums* at the vitrine.
Her smeared lipstick on his handkerchief

seems tart like the cherry on *halewat el-jeben.*
His breath reeks of marzipan when he snores.

When he coughs, halva agitates his phlegm.
I clear his pockets of sesame seeds and walnut

crumbs form his wallet. Her slithering fingers
have removed the coins, the wristwatch,

the wedding band. I have told your father,
You mustn't eat the stale eclairs that harlot sells

in her parlor. She mixes the custard with arsenic
and kills wretched souls like you in a slow death.

Shahé Mankerian

Motown and Pancakes

I'm looking for a lover
who makes me wanna
whisk milk
crack yolk
sift flour
beat butter
pour batter
grease iron skillets and
drip circles from my spoon
on a Sunday morning
to Smokey and the Temptations
Mary Wells and the Supremes we'll

shoop and shuffle
our way around
the kitchen
to back up baby love *oh baby love*
I need yas *oh oh*
I need yaas
while flames lick steel
(like a heat wave!
burning in my heart)
dropping dirty
dishes in soapy water

I wear his shirt
collar slipshod
on my shoulder

fliptoss
one handed
two handed – clap
spin and floor landed
golden brown
rounds stack
high drizzle
syrup and chocolate sauce
scoop fresh cream
fig jam and pecan
praline or whatever
we feel like

maybe we do the crossword
get stuck
across try
going down
making love
fall asleep to Stevie
this, our *shoo be doo be doo da day*
with maple on our hands
and flour in our hair.

Annette Wong

Published version, Poetry Superhighway 2011.

Muse

In search of a muse
       inspiration flowed out of you
an aesthetic for which philosophies are forged from
       words entwined to conceive poetry
on the page
       your affair
on the canvas
       our marriage
in each octave
       my anger
we unearthed an art form
       then you were gone
In search of a muse.

Damian Gonzalez

My Father's Monster Biscuits

When I was little my mother fixed most of the meals
for our family of seven but every now and then my father
would rise early on Sunday and fix breakfast.

His breakfast foods came from his Southern upbringing
bacon, eggs over easy and home made biscuits.

He was pretty good at frying bacon and eggs
but I didn't trust his baking.

I watched as he poured flour into a bowl
added baking powder, stirred in lard and water.

Watching his steel-making hands shape
large chunks of dough into biscuits, I bit my tongue
to keep from saying, *Daddy, they too big.*

In the oven the biscuits would rise until they were
big as loaves of bread but I didn't complain.

I sat at the table with the rest of my family
and attacked his monster biscuits with a knife.

They tasted pretty good with butter, syrup
and a tall glass of milk.

After breakfast our tummies would be so swollen
we could barely get up from the table.

We didn't ask for anything else to eat 'til supper time.

Hazel Clayton Harrison

National Update

(May 2018)

Breakin' News! Breakin' News!
America has morphed into a psychotic zoo,
a divisive, schizophrenic coup!
oh, say, can you see
the seedy deeds of those worshipping greed,
white men in white suits,
with sprinklings of Latinos and Blacks to boot,
who have sold their souls for thick accounts and celebrity,
oh, yes, I can see
the lies and ties to the NRA and
the dark money of billionaires
who boldly claim they only care
about their myopic views of power,
where the privileged will pillage
the last penny from a disabled child's piggy bank

and who are we to thank
for the emptiness that sank
our democratic pride into landfills of waste,
the toxic air that's brown and thick,
blind to the suffering of the homeless and sick,
those who still pimp the White House lies
about jobs and the way things never were

our ideals have been stripped away,
with nothing to believe in but doubt,
where talks about walls
distract from the moral disgust
of a nation that's lost my noble trust

Breakin' News! Breakin' News!
confront and diagnose with speed
while the country still owns a beating heart,
before we render a final autopsy
of a union that once had a spine,
but now staggers into mediocrity,

Breakin' News! Breakin' News!
I'll shout it out once more!
move swiftly! show life!
because the coroner's at the door!

Mel Donalson

Noonday Demon

Before you prepare your pyre
and set yourself ablaze

before you start your running jump
or walk calmly towards the water

before you draw the curtains
and put yourself to sleep

try, if you can,
to withstand

even a moment
longer.

Annette Wong

Notes from Music Time at the Place Where People Who Forget Live

L is for the love was made for me and you and…
My mother's legs move forward and backwards forward and backwards perfect
rhythm. Beautiful singer sways, like a Disney princess, always singing, bright red lips radiate,
nonstop smile, sweetness spreads. Mom's feet keep going as if she can still hear

the music even after the princess stops. *From Kiss Me Kate to So in Love,* mom adjusts
her pace to tempo as if dancing. Earlier she says, "not so good" when I ask her
how she is. "My kids are not ok." Gershwin playing now, it's music time again.
Getting to know you… and Don't sit under the apple tree with anyone else but me…

Some residents are clapping now. Others slump in wheelchairs, snoring
arrhythmically. *I love you for sentimental reasons. Mambo Italiano.* Song ends. One woman
keeps clapping, doesn't stop, another sings loudly, her "fellow travelers" turn
and glare at her. Do you have your wallet?" mom asks. "This girl…"

she wants to tip her. *My Funny Valentine* sings the singer. *Dancing Cheek to Cheek* mom's feet
go back and forth as if she's dancing with our Dad. Peering at her feet as if she
wonders how they do just what they do. The place they live is called Connections,
but as they lose more of themselves, they're moved to *Haven. Heaven, I'm in heaven.*

Unforgettable sings the singer. Now I'm taken
back to my lost dreams.

Carla Sameth

October Eleventh

Our home turned to ice one bitter cold night,
winter rattling the door before we knew it.
Withered witch fingers hung from the threshold
admonishing us; our foolish contentment—
fractures in the floorboards held us hostage
when our propriety became too heavy.
White breath puffed out, visible, hovering
silence where words that should have been said were not.

Damian Gonzalez

Group Photo

Off stage

Lump on her breast
I knew she would

come back home again
medical secrets exposed

push her off stage
into the wings

wrinkles sagging skin ignored
dance a slow waltz

long white silk gown
caress floor center stage

peek behind curtain
twenty two for second time

turn away from light
future picks lock

she sprints into tomorrow.

Gerda Govine Ituarte

Omen

Black bird wings
flap furiously

circles again & again
swoops up down

blue sky disappears
grey clouds gather grow

smell of rain ride cold winds
temperature drops

hail bounces on patio
flowers leaves branches

bend break against their will
downpour relentless

mud form streams
across acres of land

brave mountains hold their ground
late afternoon phone call

terminal cancer in hospice
fireplace roars

well of tears burst
flames soothe

memories bridge
her journey *home*.

Gerda Govine Ituarte

Oooh Baby Baby

If songwriters wrote songs
Without
Oooh baby baby

And
Poets wrote rhyme
Without
Oooh baby baby

And lovers made love
Without
Oooh baby baby

And
Artists made art
Without
Oooh baby baby

Where would love be
Without
Oooh baby baby?

Toni Mosley

Paradise Interrupted

Walk along marron valley trail
dwarfed by kuuchamaa
sacred mountain
>   Split in half by san diego
>   tecate mexico border

>   low lying grass crushed by
>   monster tires out of control

Earth mangled by tracks
deep enough to snap ankles
no fly zone for birds
>   At distance bright red
>   flowers soften landscape
>   joy full get closer horror

>   Red plastic shotgun casings
>   trail trash beauty moans

long gone shooters reckless
bullets graze friends home
splinter tree limbs trunks

>   Whether we look or not
>   earth mountains ancestors
>   remember.

Gerda Govine Ituarte

Poet Warrior

(for Ken Wibecan)

I once knew a man

                Wearing a kufi, a dashiki
                a necklace of cowrie shells
                he swept into the room

                his poetry was like acupuncture
                opening my chakras
                making me feel emotions
                I never knew I had

                his weapons weren't knives and guns
                but words that pierced my heart

A man who reminded me

                of some lost African tribe
                I once belonged to
                some crossroad at which
                we had once met

I once knew a man

                With lightening in his beard
                eyes that could see beneath skin
                into the heart

A man who taught me

         we are all part of a never ending
         chain of command somewhere
         between ants and God

         despite our pain and agony
         we can travel roads with
         dignity compassion humility

a poet warrior he was

I once knew a man.

Hazel Clayton Harrison

Toni Mosley

Pork Chops and Gravy

Mama's love always smelled of dinner.
On Sundays we ate the
Gospel Bird, fried chicken, mashed potatoes
Green beans and a lettuce, tomato salad

On Mondays, pork chops smothered in gravy over rice,
Green peas and a lettuce, tomato salad with carrots

We especially loved catfish Fridays with French fries and cole slaw
No salad, no vegetables

Tuesdays through Thursdays were also a delight,
Where we might have breakfast for dinner, pancakes,
Sausage and eggs, or hot dogs and hamburgers, whatever we desired.

In our house, everybody loved mama's homemade Betty Crocker
Chocolate Cake right out the box with ice cream or a tall glass of
Milk and a good family laugh.

Didn't matter to us eating chocolate cake out the box
As long as it was good.

Toni Mosley

Possibilities

In this split of the multiverse
I already have our child.

She latches readily, her small
pink fingers on my chest.

Before you lift   the lid
the cat is at once   dead
and alive.   Do you look?

Secret fear,   some quirk of biology,
Yours   *or mine?*

Before moving to Peru,
Katrina freezes her eggs.

Insurance, she says.
She is my age.

My mother reminds me of my age.
Each visit,   more lines.
Each visit,   another phantom

ache.

We grow
old together.

Annette Wong

Published version, Written Here: The Community of Writers Poetry
Review 2017.

Provincetown Morning

A morning like this one! It's 2:30 am, you
can't sleep, hour passes, another half-hour, still awake. Your head
full of words.

Sleep is a lost art when there is so much calling out
to be written. Jump out of bed at 4:00 am and a poem speeds through
chrysalis to beginning of a butterfly, or so you imagine, at 5:00 am.,

when you say it's time to go see the sunrise delicately
spreading its arms in front of the empty pier. Empty except for those few,
like you, who might want to paint the morning.

Today I paint it P-Town pink. Tomorrow I might sleep through,
while others bustle by wide awake. Then I would paint
it blue, or not at all.

Carla Sameth

Quan Âm on a Dragon

Mother shows me a lacquered painting on a plaque
of Quan Âm, bodhisattva of compassion, riding a dragon.

It is misty around the bodhisattva and the dragon.
The picture looks so real, almost like a photo.

A sacred vase in one hand and a willow branch
in the other to bless devotees with the divine nectar of life.

Mother says that she and other boat refugees saw Quan Âm as we were
fleeing Vietnam after the war in a freight boat with 2,450 refugees.

When she looked up towards Heaven, in the clouds, she saw
the bodhisattva in her white, flowing robe riding a dragon.

Mother says that the goddess was there to guide and save us
from the strong waves of the South China Sea. I should know

better than to believe her though she swears it's true.
I ask again and she nods, says really, I saw Quan Âm in the clouds

as we were escaping. I should know better than to believe her.
But, a part of me wants to believe in a bodhisattva, in compassion

riding on a mythical creature, to believe that somehow something
more than just our mere human selves wanted us to live.

Teresa Mei Chuc

"Quan Âm on a Dragon" was first published in Whitefish Review.

Annette Wong

Reckoning

Before the salon, I line my eyes;
apply concealer, shadow, rouge and gloss.
This time, I am prepared
to sit in the styling chair, where my head
floats above the cutting gown,
replicated, infinitely
in the row of mirrors in front and behind.
Call it an exercise in deception,
this covering up, I am increasingly uneasy
sitting with myself unadorned for so long.
By my feet, hair gathers quickly
in damp, black strands
wisps of calligrapher's ink.
smattered across the tile floor.
My mother hates my hair short
tells me I should wear it long, while I can.
Hers is cropped to her ears.
I watch her count the strands
she pulls from her brush.

Annette Wong

Published version, My Mane Series, Silver Birch Press 2016.

Reflection

there was a time
when time was there,
before me, calling me to
rush towards dreams not yet named,
when the days were long
and sunsets were endless thoughts

my breaths now seem shorter,
the heart beats slower but louder,
reminding me of regrets
shaped by unfulfilled desires

I am in need of synchronicity,
when past and present
still speak in harmony to future wishes,
an elusive chorus it seems,
yet each moment rife with possibilities
that serve as my sword and shield,
hoping for another day I'll get to do battle

Mel Donalson

Resistance

Rabiah, I threw a rock at your bedroom
window because you went to the movies

with the blind baker, and you didn't mind
the smell of yeast underneath his fingernails.

You allowed the bloody butcher to sit next
to you in church because he trimmed the fat

from the oxtail your mama purchased
for the stew. Yes, I threw the rock.

The schizophrenic locksmith wrote
verses from *The Prophet* on your dirty

windshield and claimed he is Gibran.
The dentist with the fake certificate

simply pulled your decaying tooth;
it's not like he healed a leper by the pool;

he didn't deserve a picnic by the reservoir.
Rabiah, I smashed your window with a rock

because your heart seemed preoccupied;
I wanted your curtains to tremble, not you.

Shahé Mankerian

Mel Donalson

Resurrection

I saw Jesus walk into the coffee shop,
his hair as dark and curly as the old testament verse,
his brown eyes catching the admiring stare of the short-haired
barista, her smile a bit more personal for him,
his laptop clutched against his side,
his stance strong and still,

his thongs brought him to the table next to mine,
his jeans as wrinkled as his shirt,
his dusky skin from a beach-long walk,
no desert miles or reflective days
but a persistent widening gaze,
his coffee black across sipping lips,

tapping his keyboard, intent in a singular gaze,
his fingers constructing a reflective prayer,
he wrote and shaped his words with an impressive ease
rising so softly, a natural warmth swirling the air
as he stared off into a place that he alone could see

when I caught his gaze, he nodded knowingly
in recognition of me, and me in recognition
of those around us who needed him most,
but all were obsessed with their own concerns
and seemed generally disconnected and unaware
that the one they were waiting to return was already there

Mel Donalson

Rhythm and Blues

I come from a
rock n roll
rhythm and blues
crap games on the floor
cops at the door
kind of family

Friday night card parties
with high yellow women
tight asses in tight dresses
cooing in the ears of men
the color of midnight

They danced as Ray Charles
pounded his keys and Billy Clubs
rapped at the door. Ray sang out
"Hey baby with the red dress on"
while cops barged in with guns drawn.

Win or lose, this was the house
of rhythm and blues

As viewed from the crack in
the door by a young daughter
somewhere Round Midnight
listening to the blues.

Toni Mosley

Rose

When I was little, my mom used to tell me not to smell roses
because the small bugs would get into my nose.
I avoided sniffing roses into adulthood.

One day, a beautiful bush of red and white
roses implored me, to take a closer look.

I leaned closer than my mom would have liked.
It happened quickly, without a thought, a waft
like honey.

I smelled again.

Then I was curious about the purple ones, the
orange ones, and the deep red ones.

Teresa Mei Chuc

Secondary Inspections

A nose, a foreign look, a memory. "They just want to know if you are Jewish," your mom says of questions about what country you came from; you know that you'll never pass for who you are. Everyone here sweats. Everyone foreign claims your face. City of Angels swelters, everyone here from somewhere else, still they ask, "Where were you born?" and "How do you say 'Hello'?" You answer fearing hatred. Fear you came by naturally after strip search and secondary inspections. Not beautiful.

"Go to New York—you'll be sought out" the statuesque, unapologetically beautiful Black, Columbian woman says. Not here, you're Toucan Sam, you're a Jew. "Angelenos look for an airbrushed affect, images of themselves," she says. Hatred for your ancestral look. "You have only a slight accent, where are you from?" Later old Armenian men shout out greetings from their balconies, ask questions you can't understand. You only know your strong nose on face

too ugly for years. For a girl. And you're hairy. White Angelenos seek their own face, lips full, not too ethnic, unless ambiguous, not too angular, no rough edges. Beautiful. Customs guards interrogate, hands grab your body. In Greece, Danish boys ask you for towels, assume you are from Parros. Jewish journalist writes story, gets tweets – his beheaded caricature rises from desire to make America white again. You are zoo animals watched by hatred.

You fear reaction to your ancestral aura. You find hidden outposts of hatred. City of Angels where everyone came from somewhere else. Yet your face looks foreign. Daily you hear, "no where are you really from?" No use saying you are second generation born in America, land of the beautiful. Your mom's answer to that was always, "They only want to know if you're Jewish." You go with your son on a field trip, "What tribe are you?" Cherokee guide asks.

"Of course we both came across the Bering Straits," he says and doesn't ask "where are you really from?" when you answer. Shows no hatred. "From Russia, Hungary, Palestine, Turkey," you say and tell him you're Jewish. Watch what hashtag you use, lest it shows up as a cross burned on your Facebook page. Maybe it's true what the Columbiana says, "Go to New York, you'd be beautiful there." Here, your Black son looks like someone they might shoot or run from.

You look like someone might be rounded up, asked "where from?" A man lingering outside 7-11, looks at you both and asks, "Egyptian?" Your son mimes the walk like Egyptian dance, your beautiful son. Later he says, "I guess there's more racism than I thought," hatred spewing out of a parking attendants mouth spits as he yells at a face that looked a lot like my son. KKK leader posts "Of course they're not white. Jews"

You're looked upon with suspicion, hatred, wondering where you're from Will they look at our faces, hear an unspoken word and ask? You wonder: In New York, will I be beautiful, will we be safe? Jew and Afro-Jew.

Carla Sameth

Published in *Unlikely Stories Mark V*, March 2018.

Severance

dazed by escapades that pushed
me to the borders of conformity,
ever present and reminding me of crushed
feelings and stormy insecurities.

which direction is the best,
which lover the final test
of who I am now and who
I am to be when compared to the rest

in many unexplained ways
I found fulfillment that avoids uncertainty,
no longer drifting with confusion,
but liberated in moments of tranquility

the many years of providing and guiding,
have brought me to the ledge of meaning,
knowing I shared all there was to offer,
avoiding bitter words and selfish scheming

giving needs *taking* from time to time,
an intersection of the human and the ideal,
and the silence hungers for the noisy phases
where the fantasy dovetails with the real

leave me here with my maddening thoughts,
where wishing cannot amend what exists,
and whenever I recall our haunting past,
your desertion will transform into a kiss

Mel Donalson

Shakshouka

Father chopped three soft tomatoes
and balanced a dangling cigarette
in his mouth. He gave his back

to the bedroom and Mother's
glaring eyes before he splattered
a lump of butter into the hot pan.

He peeled two cloves of garlic
and crushed them on the cutting
board with the heel of his palm.

"We haven't paid the mortgage,"
she taunted. He wished the radio
played Beethoven and drowned

Mother's voice like the dishes
in the sink full of dirty water.
When he felt that tightness

in his chest, he paused, leaned
against the counter to suppress
the pain. He removed his glasses

because the yolks looked blurry
in the pan like jaundiced eyeballs.
Mother didn't get to him on time.

The sizzling butter turned
the edges of the egg whites black.
A moth trapped in the cumin

container fluttered. Father
hit the linoleum tile with the salt
dish, scallions, and the spatula.

Shahé Mankerian

She Said *Leave Me Alone*

I'm reading.
I'm writing.
I'm thinking.

He said What are you making for dinner?
What are we doing tomorrow?
Have you walked the dog?

She said I don't know about dinner.
I'm doing calculus in my head.
Don't interrupt me.

He said Have you seen my glasses?
Why are you still working on this?
I'm not trying to bother you.

She said Don't come in here.
Even the kids know to leave me alone.
I can't have two thoughts.

He said, I'm your husband.
I just want to be nice to you.
Want to have a glass of wine with you.

She said, Now are you happy?
We can listen to *Rite of Spring*.
There's cherry pie.

He said, I like it when we're together.
I like it when we're having a good time.
That's what I like.

Kate Gale

Group photo

Shout

when the spotlight passes by,
no friendly touch upon my face,
I once again move in darkness,
I once more grab the edges
of my difference in this dim lit space,
filled with mornings of solitary yearnings,
and evenings where there's dark despair,
forever my passions simmering and burning,
forever striving, rising in mid-air

in a place that I call home,
away from the gazes, the scowls
of those who think they know
who I am, those who are prone
to lead me along steps they sow,
into circles they fear to walk alone.

how can I break from their grasp?
that pulling, clutching, drowning of my soul?
if it were an easy task, I would deny myself,
embrace their likeness as a way to become whole.

I stood alone in the shadow of regrets,
showered in my isolated tears,
baptized with longings and secrets,
hiding from whispers and vicious sneers.

but this melancholy has reached an end,
a new world begins where I care not
if you praise me or condescend.

pass me by if you choose,
attack me with curses and spiteful names,
I refuse to deny, to further self-abuse
to win your favor, your unfulfilling fame,
from this harbor, inside, I find my cornerstone,
to sculpt, to sing my life in infinite overtones,
my dreams and spirit a burning legacy,
an affirming shout—I'm me! I'm me!

Mel Donalson

Smelled like Seattle

Crunchy leaves today when you stepped out, moist, fresh, harkened hometown coolness. One rare February day it is cold enough you even miss the gloved scraper you used in Seattle to part the ice in wee hours of the morning. You live in LA now, your adopted city since you were in your 20's. LA the city that often sweats almost fragrant urinary scent, Eucalyptus? Or might be actual pee. Dog, cat, human, thinned out with the sun, occasional rain. Thankful prayer escapes lips here, now, your verdant life. Allow whiff of birthplace, Seattle, to bring sheer curtain of comfort, surprising this age almost 60, when all is supposed to come together: the ailments, the pleasure, the refusal to grip tightly to regrets. The willingness to look the other way, accept how it all shook out. Leave your clinging to unmet dreams behind. "At this age, nothing surprises me," you've heard this from the elders who might have twenty more years on you, counting time left. Their only response a shake of the head, a smile, a chuckle. They note the missing people who have died or disappeared, and the ones just let go of, like the dropping of calendar pages from the high above windows as was the custom in LA's City Hall just before the New Year. All this, happens as they move closer to endpoint, regrets slink sheepishly out back door, decide not to come back next year. This then, is what you wish for. Perhaps in ten years you'll know this freedom; you'll cling to nothing. Welcome it all.

Carla Sameth

Sonrise

(for Derek)

The world continually suffers and cries,
this country I claim tilting on a cornerstone of lies,
the still waters I've longed for and sought
have dried into muddy crevices filled with rot,
so many questions explode in endless cascades,
the wilted flowers of sanity that slowly fade
into shadows of unrecognizable solemn shapes,
when an elusive morality provides little escape

Into this world I thought I understood,
you arrived with the innocence of your golden boyhood,
your heart shaped by wonder, an intellect divinely drawn,
the color of your skin tinted by a summer's dawn,
and as you became a man with your singular strength,
I've been restored with hope to an immeasurable length,
when I suffer sorrows and anxieties that never seem to cease,
your mere presence is a blessing of soothing peace

Mel Donalson

Spicy Punishment

Mother, I know why you rubbed the pork
with Aleppo pepper. On the parchment paper,

your red thumbprints lingered as proof.
Your generous flakes permeated more

in the muhammara than the pomegranate molasses.
When Father fell asleep, you cheated

and added extra pinches of pepper
in the manti sauce. The recipe didn't call for it;

Salade Russe didn't need it. I couldn't taste
the cumin in baba ghanoush. My lebneh

sandwich dripped with crimson olive oil
because of anger. At that age, your fights

with father lasted for weeks. We didn't deserve
your backhanded retaliation. Our tongues

didn't have to burn until you made peace
and the bamya returned to being bland.

Shahé Mankerian

Teresa Mei Chuc

Spring Poem

The flowers are blooming
and so are the bruises
on her face
purple and pink like showy penstemon
and there is no where she could go

The bruises on her arm
the deep violet of prickly pear fruits
tender to the touch

The flowers are blooming
around her tent on the hillside
overlooking the freeway
sunflowers, each branch
carrying light

The robins, mockingbirds and blue jays
are singing
as his fist punches her

The flowers are blooming
fuchsia red
fairy duster red
on her skin
and there is no where she could go.

Teresa Mei Chuc

Dedicated to our grandmothers, mothers, sisters and daughters experiencing houselessness.
#SheDoes deserve shelter, protection and compassion

Standoff

She pushes her red chair
away from the table and steps down.
We warn her not to walk away.

She does. She wants to boycott
the leftover okra and sticky rice.
We won't give her what she wants:

corn flakes, Nutella on pita,
or slices of cucumber dipped in lebni.
We send her to her room without dinner,

but that's not her punishment.
The ladder to her bunk bed creaks.
She tucks herself in. "Who's going

to read me a book?" she calls out.
We don't answer. We stare
at her room in silence.

Shahé Mankerian

Tall Poppy

She walks around with her head in air.
Like she's somebody.

Who is she?
She came to town, built a library.

Who cares?
Who needs a library?

We have our own books.
We have our own parties.

She's never invited me to one of her parties.
Well, she invited me once.

Once I got there, she never talked to me.
Never offered me a glass of wine.

I do not understand it. Her brain must be
a crowded little place telling her, You're terrific!

She's fallen flat on her face now.
She'll be down for a while.

I used to think I could help her. I wanted to sit her down
say, slow down. Do what I say. You'll be okay.

I wanted to say, Keep your head down.
In this town, they'll eat you alive.

But she kept laughing and marching around
like she knew everything.

Now that's she's flat on her face,
I hope she learns her lesson.

I hope she learns to keep her mouth shut.
She thought she was the tall poppy around here.

People like her get their houses burned down.
They get stung by a buzz of bees.

Their heads are cut off.
Goodbye tall poppy.

Kate Gale

Shahé Mankerian

The Boy in the Elevator

Because of the bomb blast, we lost electricity.
Trapped between floors, the feebleminded
delivery boy banged on the metal door.

No one moved because another bomb
exploded, and the windowpanes of the bank
building shattered. "Eat the feta cheese

in the grocery bag," Mama shouted,
"before hungry rats keep you company."
Crossfire of machine guns syncopated

the nightfall. We saw the curling smoke
from the dome of the Armenian church,
and an ambulance smashed into a lamppost.

A rocket struck the rooftop water tanks.
The searchlight masqueraded as the moon.
We heard the cables creak and remembered

the boy in the elevator.

Shahé Mankerian

The Boy on the Crates

In the alley behind the mosque,
he climbed a stack of milk crates
because he wanted to see

the forest behind the wall, the nest
of the tortured bulbul, the chocking
clock surrounded by cornhusks,

and militiamen who slept
with machine guns as their malign
mistresses. The coffee-colored

prostitute hid behind the pulled
curtains because the boy
on the rickety crates used her

bedroom like his personal cinema.
He cried when he saw a stray
bullet kills a beggar by the bridge.

In a dream, the tower of crates
toppled, and the stoic, indifferent
God fell from the sky into quicksand.

Shahé Mankerian

The Children

Night bays at the moon
while children dream

Ride polka dot ponies
across bluest sky

Clouds play hide & seek
sun rays brighten horizon

No match for rainbows
eagle hovers wings slice air

Swoop down up gone
hear roar of airplane

Snow dust mountaintops
trees rocks flowers yearn

For spring as bunnies play
children wake up hugging pillow

Polka dots cover bed
only they can see.

Gerda Govine Ituarte

The Dead & The Living

violent
shadows
impressed
upon
our
graves
sharp
black
and
cold
cast
from
those
we
left
on
the
surface
angry and alone

Damian Gonzalez

Published in Altadena Poetry Review / Anthology 2016.

Hazel Clayton Harrison

The Drinking Gourd

All I know about the stars I learned from Harriet.

Fix yo' eyes on the Big Dipper, she said.
        Follow the handle of that ole' drinkin' gourd
til you sees the North Star.
        Follow it cross the Ohio River.
Don't look back now.
        Keep on goin' all the way to Canada
if you have to.

Hazel Clayton Harrison

The Final Act

*(for Hannah Ahlers, 34-years-old, one of the 58 people killed in
The Las Vegas shooting, October 2017)*

It was the third day, a resurrection
of a melody composed of an evil conceiving,
staccato beats raining over the intersection
of Route 91 and a starry October evening

She waited for it to come—the country cadence,
with rhythms swirling warmly as a peaceful cloud,
but the comfort was jolted by chords of confusion,
a tempo of chaos splintering the running crowd

the shell pierced her spine as she stumbled in fear
her arm caught beneath the weight of a fallen man,
his face shattered beneath bloody strands of hair
his single eye staring, attempting to understand

losing the notes to the life she knew,
her breath fading under a crescendo of dissonance,
accepting there would be no tomorrow to sing,
she surrendered to a concerto of death and irreverence

Mel Donalson

The Gamble

In the picture, my college roommate
and I sandwich a young man
whose name I've since forgotten.
Jon, perhaps, though I can't remember
if that was short for Jonathan.
It was freshman year, Casino Night.
She wears a strappy sequined dress,
me, a black strapless number, a lace choker
around my neck. Jon (I've decided that's his name)
was her date. I went alone,
stopping first for a drink in a friend's room
some concoction mixed in the shower, poured
into a red cup. I crossed
the street to the neighboring dorm
to the cafeteria masquerading
as a Vegas casino, strewn
with confetti and monopoly money,
girls wearing fake furs, boys pretending to puff
paper cigars, black jack dealt
on the same tables we ate off
trays during the week.
I hadn't thought of this night
in some time, went in search
of my roommate in old photos before
her wedding, and was reminded of us
at eighteen, rolling dice, doubling down,

flirting with all odds,
knowing they were inconsequential
but nonetheless refusing
to fold.

Annette Wong

Published version, Altadena Poetry Review 2017.

The Only Way You Can Leave

It is easier for a camel to go through the eye of a needle than for a rich
man to enter into the kingdom of God (Matthew 19:24)

The rich man has many mansions but refuses
to house the poor.

The homeless woman shares her crust of bread
with strangers.

With which one would you want to go to the Kingdom of God?
Don't envy the rich.

The only way you can leave this house is
empty handed.

Hazel Clayton Harrison

Kate Gale

The Other

We drink ice water.
Mother stares at me across the table.
Thirty-three years apart. Strangers.

> When Minerva found Medusa raped in her temple by Neptune,
> she cursed Medusa, tearing away her beauty, hair to snakes.

Mother orders seared ahi, then sends it to be cooked.
Married thirty years, leaf thin.
We pass story fragments.

> A woman without a story is no woman at all.
> Medusa, a terrible woman, feared but powerless.

What does the word "forgive" mean?
That it's all right?
That it didn't happen?

> Medusa was in a different story after the rape.
> From virgin beauty to monster.

You leave and you are other.
Without God, you are other.
Outside the great chain of being.

Other.
Mother tells me God is watching me.
That California will heave into the Pacific.

We will all be swimmers. We will have boats.
My life is the building of a lifeboat, then a raft.
From my sailboat, I can hardly see Mother on the shore.

Kate Gale

The Police Station

011419 955pm

I vaguely recall my younger sisters trying to pull me to my feet after I had fainted from the site of daddy. As I stood, mama began telling me who to call. In a haze I stumbled to the kitchen phone and dialed "O" for operator to make an emergency call to the Burnside Police Station, then looked on the slip of paper scotch taped to the wall that listed important names and numbers searching for dad's mom and dad and sister and brother; and although I wasn't sure why, I also phoned our family doctor.

Soon our small apartment was cramped with family members, the police, the doctor and a few black news reporters. The police ask mama questions about dad's suicide, none of which she could answer clearly after a night of heavy drinking. I was the one with the answers but no one asked me any questions. Mama and I are still wearing night clothes when the officers tell her they want to take us to the station for questioning. As though I were an adult, I answered the police with a "yes, we'll go to the station after we change into street clothes." After changing out of our night clothes, we followed the officers to their car. With sirens blasting and red lights flashing we are put in the back seat behind the two burly officers who together fill the front seat as they sat shoulder to shoulder, hat to hat, window to window with no space between them. When we arrive at the Burnside Station, mama and I are escorted to a small interrogation room and wait for the officers to return after checking in with their police captain. The interrogation room held a rectangular table with four metal chairs along with a blanket of hot air that the whining window fan could not dismantle.

It was Monday, September 1st, 4 am and 90 degrees.

As we wait for the officers, I do a mental review of the night's events. I don't think my mother is prepared to answer any official questions, so I decide that I will answer for her.

Toni Mosley

The Tattoo

She chose it
as a reminder
this dark green spiral
of text:

Nou led.
Nou la.*

We are ugly.
But we are here.

She showed me
where it was etched, across
the pale white
of her inner wrist.

Annette Wong

*Haitian proverb.

Damian Gonzalez

Tuol Sleng*

When the power went,
there had been rain for five days,
scattering the hawkers, the *motos*,
the men sprawled in their *tuktuks*.
Ants flecked the rambutan plucked
from a wet market stall,
days shy of ripe.

I live behind the Genocide Museum. I wrote home.
It sounds grimmer than it is.

It wasn't the spattered tiles
that got to me most,
or the whites of eyes captured
on camera, the metal beds
on which bodies were strung—but the thought—
of each prisoner's last glimpse
of sun, ruptured, through the shutters
and perforated walls
before the blindfolds, the transport,
fifteen kilometers to *Choeung Ek*,
the Killing Fields, where speakers hung
from The Magic Tree** blaring:

Children, do not forget the fresh blood of our soldiers and
Children, forever remember the revolution!

Now, darkness. New sounds audible,
without the percussive rain and hum of motors:
ceramic on tin, the neighbors' dinner utensils
set to rest. In the alley, children
with candles, laughing. The patter
of hands on smooth surfaces, the collective search
for something to light.

Annette Wong

* Tuol Sleng, also known as Security Prison (S-21), was a former high school in Phnom Penh, Cambodia, which the Khmer Rouge turned into an execution center. Prisoners who were not killed at S-21 were transported to the Killing Fields for execution. It is now a Genocide Museum.
** The Magic Tree is a tree in the *Choeung Ek* killing fields upon which the Khmer Rouge strung loudspeakers that played propaganda and music as victims were being executed.

Published version, Altadena Poetry Review 2017.

Gerda Govine Ituarte

137

Two by Four

Hope   Humanity
Justice   Truth

                 Hijacked   Shackled
                 Arrogance   Greed

Blind   Obedience
Ignites   Fear

                 Ignorance   Squats
                 Freedom   Pivots

Gerda Govine Ituarte

Unmoored

is what I feel. If nothing compares to a work this intense, that of raising
children, where am I now? Left trenches. Smoke clears. Alone. Seemingly.
They never really belong to us. (Thank you Kahlil Gibran.)

Without knowing you—Mother who carries her own water— I couldn't face
this vast expanse, but for knowing: You survived.
Walked through fire, there is no greater.
And you: whole again.

I am not there. Yet.

This morning I woke up with this knowledge:
Fear is the engine that pushes the car that will run you over.
Don't be afraid to slap me. But I don't know if it will help.

How many days since the kitty litter was changed?
Since I've watered my plants?
Since I've flung words onto paper?
Since I have seen my mom? Who still remembers me today.
But might not tomorrow.

Gardenia from the big flowered Mexican pot, dead…gone.
Every year it bloomed before, flower behind my ear, fragrant gift
to beautiful woman

Fear is the engine that pushes the car that will run you over.
Son calls. Love You Mom.
This is the perfume that matches the gardenia that frees your soul.

Carla Sameth

Warm Water

I was thirty when I met my father for the first time.
I shook his hand and said,
"I'm running late for a flight but maybe we can chat the next time we meet."
He replied,
"I'm sure we have a lot to talk about."
I saw him again four years later
in Miami.
Neither of us spoke much.
I remember him standing in the warm waters of south beach,
water to his knees, smiling,
and I tried to smile too
but he was just so ordinary.
I thought, it wasn't worth the energy
to smile for someone so average—
must have been the same thought he had when I was a baby.
Interesting,
genetics maybe…

Damian Gonzalez

Carla Sameth

Where I'm From

I am from slugs and bumblebees,
mildew, Lake Washington, Puget Sound and "the mountain is out"
I am from pick up games
(football, baseball, basketball)
Peter Collin' s knees mashing my lip split when I rush

I am from classrooms made of portables
that fill the playground and rites of passage girl fights, "tear her hair out"
Only one not Black in my Brownie Troop
I am Norris Washington's hero in fourth grade
They called me Sammy Boy

I'm from Brown, Black, Yellow Skin classmates fill Mrs. Kumata's classroom.
Safety. Mock Presidential Election: Larry Rock –plays George Wallace,
I'm Eldridge Cleaver
Fourth grade class bully Marvin
in penitentiary now for rape; Found Jesus
I'm first chair trumpet player, best fourth grade girl baseball player

I am from Mother's Father: jaded Russian revolutionary garment worker
Failed capitalist, ballroom dancer
From Father's Mother: Grandma Stella journalist on horseback,
wore IUD earrings
Took buses south to Guatemala.
Stranger gave her dirty magazines to read

Flung out to the suburbs, we are strangers
Strong noses, sharp features, olive skin, always asked what country from?
In a sea of white faces, little noses, blue eyes, engineers and quiet dinner tables
They taunt me, Toucan Sam, last picked for team by sixth grade
Write my way through it
Letters journey to cousin pen pal
Share stories savory bedlam, throttled love, existential angst
Lifeboat. Rescued.

Still Sammy Boy

Carla Sameth

Published Hometown Pasadena, July 2017

144

White Roses on Steroids

Oh you uncontainable white roses on steroids, you knocked me over when I stepped out today. The puffy pampas, the scarlet bougainvillea, the Lily of the Nile, the tall swaying purple Pride of Madeira. The scent of sage, rosemary, jasmine and some vague urine like odor massage my nose and I wander out to kiss the sky and whisper thank you, thank you, thank you. The wild unkemptness of it all is what wakes me up. A wet Southern California winter gone amok has saved us once again. If you began to think it was all about smog and traffic and no work and dying addicts, tent cities and no retirement, think again. Look up as you walk out. And hope that somewhere the lone sprig of color pokes out of the sidewalk cracks, even where you can't smell hope.

Carla Sameth

Wildfire Season

Ash falls on a wooded labyrinth of twisted roots, stumps, and scorched earth.
Willows once wept here
and the ruins used to resemble homes,
where a wiry child unearthed a muse, in art, in music, in words—
all because of a kiss on the cheek, that one time.
The past is petrified
and a ghost floats aimlessly on dead land
in search of love
by way of time travel.
The hues here once painted a story of joyful youth,
of a cheerful adolescence,
but are now violent and unsettling.
This is the place of your dreams, of your ambition,
and it has been distilled down to abstraction—
The wind blows hot and howls a dirge just for you.
Lament—oh child, lament the injustice of a wildfire.

Damian Gonzalez

Writing

To be a writer
is to be bold
and sometimes holy.

Boldness has genius, magic and power.
Holy is reverent, blessed and moral.

Today my muse assures me that
this poem is
genuine, magical and
powerfully bold.

Perhaps tomorrow my writing
will be Holy.

What I know for certain
writing truth painfully sharp
I bleed.

Toni Mosley

You Won't Amount to Much

A woman with no need for men
is a woman to be feared.

They said, "You won't amount to much."
"You'll never go to heaven."

You are the flat part of Earth.
God's hands cannot find you.

As it turns out, you won't amount to much if
    you're fat.
    you're ugly

    you don't come from a good family.
    you're fighting all the time.

    you're differently abled.
    you're different.

    you don't play by the rules.
    you think you make the rules.

    you're squeamish about smiling at men.
    you're squeamish about men.

    you can't cook and serve.
    you can't win and please.

you aren't a pleasure model.
you aren't a model of pleasure.

you don't shut your mouth.
you don't open your mouth.

you had something bad happen to you and
you can't shut up about it.

Shut up. Lie down. There's a good girl.
All we ask for is your life.

Your body. Your silence.
Don't you want to go to Heaven?

Don't you want to be one of those girls
we talk about and smile?

Kate Gale

Group collage

Pasadena Rose Poets Bio

Teresa Mei Chuc is the Altadena Poet Laureate Editor-in-chief (2018 to 2020). She is the author of three books of poetry, *Red Thread* (Fithian Press, 2012), *Keeper of the Winds* (FootHills Publishing, 2014) and *Invisible Light* (Many Voices Press, 2018). Her poetry is in the anthology *Inheriting the War: Poetry and Prose by Descendants of Vietnam Veterans and Refugees.* Teresa's chapbook of poetry *How One Loses Notes and Sounds* was published in 2016. *Nuclear Impact: Broken Atoms in Our Hands Anthology (symphonic voices of 163 poets around the world)* was published by her publishing company, Shabda Press in 2017.

Mel Donalson received his Ph.D. from Brown University, and has been a professor at Bates College, UC-Santa Barbara, Pasadena City, and UCLA. He served as editor of two texts: Cornerstones: An Anthology of African American Literature (1996), and the Encyclopedia of 20TH Century African American Literature (2007). His critical books include Black Directors in Hollywood (2003), Masculinity in the Interracial Buddy Film (2006), and Hip Hop in American Cinema (2007). In 2017 Donalson published his poetry collection, Revelations, and he wrote, directed, and published his stage play, Shout. He wrote three novels: The River Woman (1988), Communion (2012), and The Third Woman (2018). As a screenwriter and filmmaker, he wrote, produced, and directed the short films, A Room Without Doors (1998) and Performance (2009).

Kate Gale is an author, poet, librettist, and Managing Editor of Red Press and she is the author of five poetry collections. Recent works are *Goldilocks Zone,* (New Mexico Press 2014) and *Echo Light,* (Red Mountain Press 2014). She is the editor of the Los Angeles Review. Articles, poems and fiction have been published in *Gargoyle, Oberon, Rattle, Eclipse, Poems & Plays and Quarterly West.*

Damian Gonzalez is an artist, writer, and award-winning filmmaker. He was sponsored by the Creative Artists Agency to attend both the Sundance Film Festival and the Karlovy Vary Film Fest near Prague as an "Emerging talent." In 2014, he co-produced PoetryPalooza, a Southern California touring open mic. That same year, he co-created an interactive art installation entitled, "The King is Dead" for the La Puente Art-Walk. His writing has led him to work in various creative capacities in the film industry at NBC Universal, Fox Searchlight and Bad Robot studios. His work, whether in art, poetry, or filmmaking is often aimed at exploring narratives that feature identities transitioning through relationship trauma. His poetry appeared in the 2017 Altadena Poetry Review Anthology.

Hazel Clayton Harrison is the Altadena Poet Laureate for Community Events (2018-2020). She was born in the Deep South into a family of artists. To escape the poverty and terror of Jim Crow, her parents moved her and her brother to Ohio in the early 1950s. Influenced by them, Hazel dreamed of becoming a writer. She received her M.ED from Kent State University and pursued a career as an educator while writing poetry and short stories. In the 1980s her works began to appear in journals. Her work has been widely published in anthologies including, Grandfathers, A Rock Against the Wind, Altadena Poetry Review, and Coiled Serpent. Currently, she operates JAH Light Media, a publishing consulting firm. Her memoir, Crossing the River Ohio, is available on Amazon.

Gerda Govine Ituarte, Ed.D. is the author of Poetry Within Reach in Unexpected Places (2018), Future Awakes in Mouth of Now (2016), Alterations |Thread Light Through Eye of Storm (2015), and Oh, Where is My Candle Hat? (2012). She established the Pasadena Rose Poets in 2016 and in 2017 created poetry readings at Pasadena City Council meetings. She read her poetry in Escondido and El Cajon City Council meetings. Her poetry was featured in exhibits at Art Produce, California Center for the Arts Museum, El Gatito Gallery, and the New Americans Museum.

Her poetry is included in the Altadena Poetry Review, Coiled Serpent, In Flight Magazine, Journal of Modern Poetry, Ms Aligned and Spectrum. She received a B.S. and M.A. from New York University and an M.A. and Ed.D. from Teachers College, Columbia University.

Shahé Mankerian is the principal of St. Gregory Hovsepian School in Pasadena. His manuscript, *History of Forgetfulness*, has been a finalist at the Bibby First Book Competition, the Crab Orchard Poetry Open Competition, the Quercus Review Press Poetry Book Award, and the White Pine Press Poetry Prize. In 2018, *Sum* literary journal nominated Mankerian's poem "In Twos" for the Pushcart Prize. Recently, two online publications, *Border Crossing* and *Cahoodaloodaling*, have nominated Mankerian's poems for the 2018 Best of the Net. Shahé received the 2017 Editors' Prize from MARY: A Journal of New Writing.

Toni Mosley has been writing since age 12. As a former nonprofit executive, she was responsible for telling stories about her organization and its constituents through the creation of brochures and grant proposal writing. Retired in 2013 from the nonprofit sector, she has now become a professional writer of confessional poetry and is currently at work on her memoir, Dead Flies on the Window Sill, a hybrid of poetry, prose and essays about growing up in a chaotic household. Mosley's work has been featured in the Pasadena Hometown News and the Altadena Poetry Review Anthology 2019. As a member of the poetry ensemble, The Pasadena Rose Poets, she has shared her poetry and growing-up stories on the stage at the Walt Disney Concert Hall as well as at schools, libraries and the Barnes & Noble Bookstores throughout the San Gabriel Valley.

Carla Sameth is a writer living in Pasadena. Her debut memoir, One Day on the Gold Line, was published on July 18, 2019. Her work appears in a variety of literary journals and anthologies including: Collateral Journal, The Nervous Breakdown, Anti-Heroin Chic, Brevity Blog, Brain, Child, Narratively, Longreads, Mutha Magazine, Full Grown People, Angels

Flight Literary West, Tikkun, Entropy, Pasadena Weekly, and La Bloga. Carla was selected to be a 2019 Pride Poet with the City of West Hollywood and was a fall 2016 PEN In The Community Teaching Artist. She taught creative writing to incarcerated youth through WriteGirl, at the Los Angeles Writing Project, California State University Los Angeles and with Southern New Hampshire University. Carla has an MFA in Creative Writing (Latin America) from Queens University.

Annette Wong is working on a first collection of poems. Her work has been supported by the AWP Writer-to-Writer Mentorship Program, the Bread Loaf Writers' Conference, Community of Writers at Squaw Valley, VONA, and Writing Workshops Los Angeles. She is currently the Rona Jaffe Foundation Graduate Fellow at Warren Wilson College, where she is pursuing an MFA. Her work has appeared or is forthcoming in *Poetry Northwest*, *Waxwing*, and *Lantern Review*. Annette holds a B.A. in History from Yale University and a J.D. from the University of Southern California Gould School of Law. She lives in Los Angeles, where she teaches meditation and practices law.

* * * * * * * * * * * *

Photographer Alfred Haymond

Los Angeles native and longtime Altadena resident, Alfred Haymond, continues to distinguish himself as an accomplished photographer. His images are consistently on display and part of installations throughout the San Gabriel Valley and greater Westside area. Lauded for both his collaborative and solo works in exhibits such as - "Black Men Shoot" (Alkebu-lan Cultural Center 2017), "Celebrating Diversity Through Photography" (Cook Art Gallery 2018), Pasadena's annual "Observations in Black" (Citywide since 2017), the film noir inspired, "Tales of Pasadena" (Jackie Robinson Center, Art Night, 2019), and "Convergence @ The Metaphor" (Metaphor Club, Los Angeles 2019), Alfred Haymond offers the viewer a glimpse of his seemingly vintage composition style and nostalgic approach to the medium. "When asked about his ardent fascination with black & white photography, Alfred readily explains; *It's just where my head is at. It's thought provoking to the eye and therapeutic to the mind.*" Alfred can be reached at *www.ObservationalPhotography.com*

www.ingramcontent.com/pod-product-compliance
Lightning Source LLC
Chambersburg PA
CBHW022132080426
42734CB00006B/325

* 9 7 8 0 9 6 0 0 9 3 1 3 7 *